Learn to Make

kawaii

Origami

Supercute
Projects for Easy
Folding Fun

CHRISSY PUSHKIN

THUNDER BAY
P·R·E·S·S

Contents

So much fun awaiting!

Introduction 4

Tools & Techniques 4

Kawaii Art Style 6

Basic Origami Folds 6

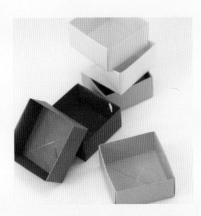

Masu Box
8

Kawaii Envelopes
11

Water Balloon
15

Tea Bag
18

Tea Bag Envelopes
22

Cute Purse
27

Masu Box 8

Kawaii Envelopes 11

Water Balloon 15

Tea Bag 18

Tea Bag Envelopes 22

Cute Purse 27

Cat & Dog Hearts
31

Cactus
39

Round Pot
43

Ice-Cream Cone
49

Sushi Roll Boxes
57

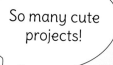

So many cute projects!

Welcome!

Introduction

THE WORD *KAWAII* TRANSLATES SIMPLY AS "CUTE" in Japanese, but it is now used to describe a certain style that is adorable, bright, and friendly.

So how do you make your origami look Kawaii? The end result of any origami model can be Kawaii if you choose a pretty pattern or color! Each of the origami models included in this book can look Kawaii if you use the paper provided, or you can make them with paper of other colors and patterns to produce any style you like. For instance, using red, blue, and white can give you a nautical style; black, purple, and red will give projects a gothic feel; or if you want something that looks rustic and natural, use brown, white, and gray papers. Those are just a few examples; there is honestly no limit to what can be created with origami.

All of the models included can be given as gifts, and in some cases, made into jewelry, so even when they aren't "practical" they can still serve a purpose! There are several new origami models in this book that have not been seen anywhere else. These include the following projects: Kawaii envelopes (page 11), tea bag (page 18), cute purse (page 26), cactus (page 39), and sushi roll boxes (page 57). Models such as the cat & dog hearts (page 31) and ice-cream cone (page 49) in particular represent the Kawaii theme and style of origami models that I enjoy designing the most. You will also find a few traditional origami models that are great for beginners to fold, such as the masu box (page 8) and the water balloon (page 15), which is lovely to hang up and super fun to make as well!

I hope you enjoy creating Kawaii origami!

Tools & Techniques

Before we start our extremely fun Kawaii origami projects, there are a couple of basic tools and techniques that you will need to start, and some that come in handy when you want to make variations of the basic origami project.

Paper

All you really need for most origami models is . . . paper! There are quite a few different kinds of paper that you can use. The most popular and easy-to-use paper for origami is known as *kami* paper. Kami paper is thin, crisp, and easy to fold but doesn't rip easily like regular printer paper. You can find kami paper in packs of 50, 100, or 500 in most craft stores and many places online. Depending on your budget, you can

Color me in!

get inexpensive packs for under $3 or higher-quality papers that cost a good deal more. Another paper that is commonly used in origami is *chiyogami* paper, which is traditional Japanese paper that is printed in a countless array of beautiful patterns and colors. But you don't need specialized paper to make origami. There are lots of different types of paper you can fold with, including some that you may already have around your house. Wrapping paper, pages from a magazine or newspaper, fancy handmade paper, and even parchment paper used for baking all work! When you first begin learning origami, it helps to use paper you don't mind throwing away so you can experiment without worrying about wasting special or pricey paper. This could be cheap kami paper or even just printer paper that you cut into a square. Included in this book are 70 sheets of 6 × 6-inch (15 × 15-cm) origami paper to get you started, which is both the most common size of origami paper and the one needed for all of the projects included in the following pages. Ten of the sheets have fun patterns that you can color in with colored pencils, crayons, or markers.

Stickers

Want to make your models more Kawaii? Use your imagination and turn any, or all, of the origami creations into fun and whimsical Kawaii characters. Use the included stickers to transform your paper art into fully realized animals, characters, and personas!

Here are some ways you can add expressions to your projects:

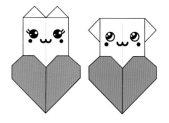

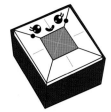

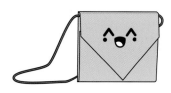

Other Tools

A few tools can make origami easier to do. I suggest making an origami tool kit that includes:

- A folding tool, or "bone folder," which is used to flatten creases.
- A ruler and a pencil, because some models require that you measure something.
- Scissors, or another cutting tool.
- A paper scoring tool to make precision folds.
- A chopstick to round the edges of the paper.
- Glue to reinforce a box or attach decorations like glitter and ribbons.

Kawaii Art Style

Kawaii is a Japanese concept that started in the 1970s. The word itself translates to "cute" in English. Although the word *Kawaii* in Japanese can be used to describe almost anything that is "cute," ranging from clothing to jewelry, it is commonly used to describe the immensely popular and immediately identifiable art style seen in emojis and characters like Hello Kitty and Pokémon. Like most art styles, there are countless interpretations of what is considered "Kawaii," the common attributes to this pop style are simple black lines, rounded characters with a youthful appearance, and the use of pastel colors and simple facial expressions on characters with oversized heads on top of small bodies.

Basic Origami Folds

Throughout the book, you will see symbols that represent common origami folds in the instructional diagrams. Always be sure to align the fold sides as precisely as possible in each step before moving on to the next. Hold and rotate the origami model according to the instructional diagrams, and use whichever fingers are the most comfortable for you and that allow you to make a correct fold. Over time, you will develop a preference. Remember, practice makes perfect, and after a couple of trials and a few errors, you will soon be folding like an origami pro.

> **FOLDING TIP**
> When following an origami diagram, it helps to look at the next step in order to see how the model should look after completing the step you are currently on.

FOLD
Fold the paper in the direction of the arrow.

VALLEY FOLD
This is one of the basic origami folds. It indicates you should fold the paper *over* itself to make a crease so the paper bends downward, resembling a "V" shape or "valley."

MOUNTAIN FOLD
Like the valley fold, this is another basic origami fold. It indicates you should fold the paper *behind* itself to make a crease so the paper bends upward, resembling a "mountain" peak.

DOUBLE FOLD
Fold the paper two times.

FOLD AND UNFOLD
Fold once and then unfold.

TIP
You can find video tutorials online for some of the origami projects in this book!

Visit: paperkawaii.com and select origami instructions/videos tutorials to view them.

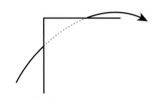

FOLD BEHIND
Fold the paper behind itself.

FLIP OVER
Flip the origami model over from either its front to its back or vice versa as indicated.

ROTATE
Rotate the origami model in the direction indicated.

INFLATE
Blow air into the origami model.

PRESS OR PUSH
Firmly press or push on the fold where indicated.

CUT
Using scissors, cut where indicated.

CLOSE-UP VIEW
Indicates an enlarged view on a particular area of the origami model.

STAR SYSTEM
You will see stars next to each project, with one star being the easiest and four stars representing the most advanced. In addition, the projects are arranged sequentially, starting with easier origami models to build your folding skills as you go.

DIFFICULTY:  = Easiest ⟶ ☆☆☆☆ = Hardest

Masu Box

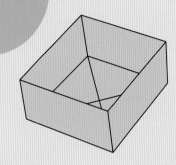

This traditional origami masu box is probably the easiest project in this book. Besides being easy, it is a very good model to start with because it incorporates lots of different folding techniques. Masu boxes were originally used to measure rice, but nowadays serve lots of different uses such as storage for little cute things, a thoughtful gift box, or a stand for an adorable figurine—and it is fun to fold.

DIFFICULTY:

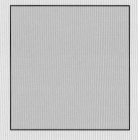

1. Start with your paper color side up.

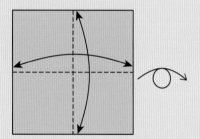

2. Fold the paper in half and unfold, then fold the paper in half in the other direction and unfold.

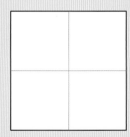

3. Flip the paper over to the other side.

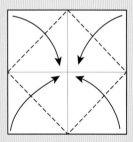

4. Fold each corner to the middle.

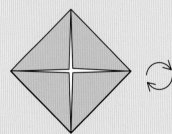

5. Rotate the paper.

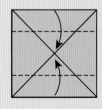

6. Fold the top and bottom edges to the center, making sure the edges are aligned.

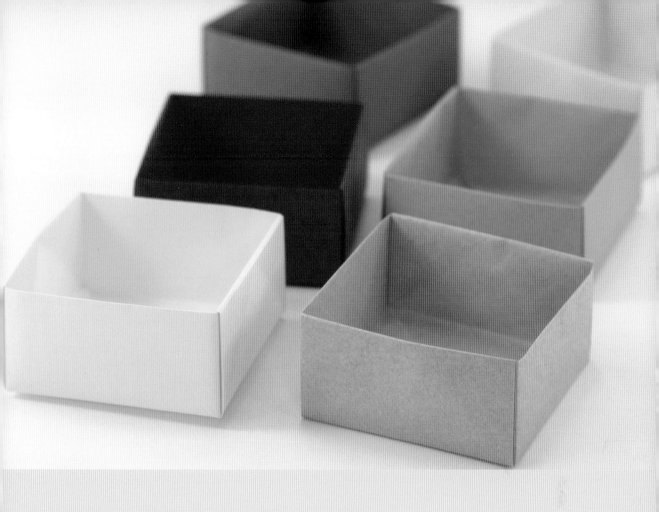

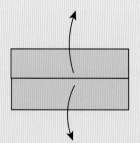

7. Unfold the top and bottom flaps.

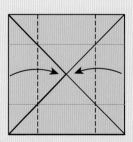

8. Fold the left and right edges to the center.

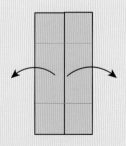

9. Unfold the left and right flaps.

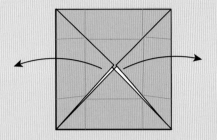

10. Open the left and the right sections.

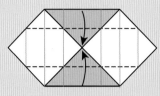

11. Refold the top and bottom edges to the center.

12. This is what it should look like.

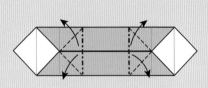

13. Using the existing diagonal creases, open up the middle section.

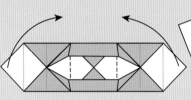

14. Lift up the left and right ends, making the model become three-dimensional.

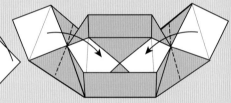

15. Continue to push the left and the right sides of the model together.

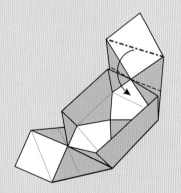

16. Fold the right end over and inside the model, locking it into place.

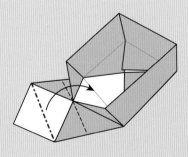

17. Repeat on the left side to complete your masu box.

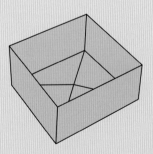

Kawaii Envelopes

These little envelopes are as easy to make as they are cute! They are great for party invitations, as their rounded corners allow for lots of ways to decorate the envelopes depending on the occasion. The envelopes can also be decorated like mochi, which is a round Japanese dessert—or you can draw or use stickers to create a cute emoji face, donut, or cake on them!

DIFFICULTY:

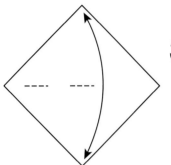

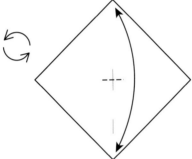

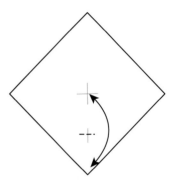

1. Create small horizontal creases by bringing the bottom point up to the top point and pressing your nail lightly across the paper where indicated.

2. Rotate the paper so that the creases you made in the previous step are on the lower section, and create another small horizontal crease in the center.

3. Bring the bottom point up to the middle, creating a small horizontal crease in the lower section. You should now have two plus-shaped creases.

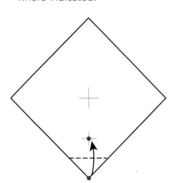

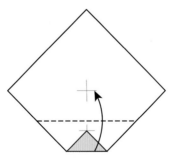

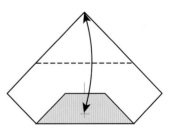

4. Fold the bottom point up to the middle of the lower plus-shaped crease.

5. Fold the bottom edge up to the middle crease.

6. Fold the top point down to the lower plus-shaped crease and unfold.

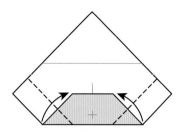

7. Fold the bottom left and right edges up diagonally.

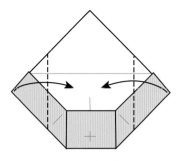

8. Fold the left and right edges inward, using the layer underneath as a guide.

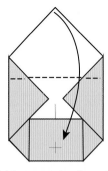

9. Fold the top point down. It should reach the lower plus-shaped crease.

10. Now you've got a super-cute Kawaii envelope!

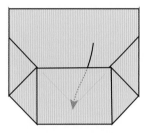

11. You can insert the point inside the envelope to secure it.

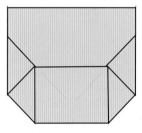

12. Here is what a closed Kawaii envelope looks like.

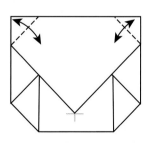

13. To make a rounded envelope, fold the top left and right corners diagonally inward and unfold.

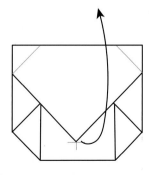

14. Unfold the top flap.

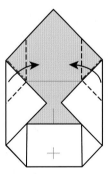

15. Fold the left and right points inward, creating new vertical creases where indicated.

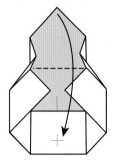

16. Refold the top flap down.

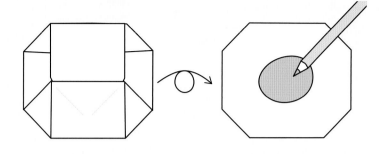

17. You can secure the envelope by inserting the point back into the pocket.

18. Flip the envelope over to the other side, and draw whatever you like here!

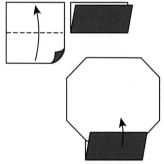

19. You can even make an onigiri rice ball by just folding a small sheet of black paper in half . . .

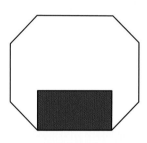

20. . . . and gluing the black paper to the envelope!

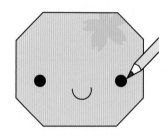

21. Make a Japanese mochi by using pastel paper and drawing a cute face or adding stickers!

So cute!

Check out the egg!

Water Balloon

This traditional origami water balloon is easy to make, and you can use it as a hanging decoration or a round object such as an apple. What makes this origami model extra fun is that you have to blow into it to make it take shape!

WASABI VARIATION PAPER SIZE: 3 × 3 inches (7.5 × 7.5 cm)

DIFFICULTY:

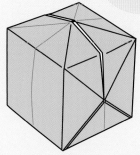

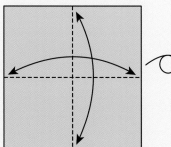

1. Starting colored side up, fold the paper in half from top to bottom and unfold, then fold the paper in half from left to right and unfold.

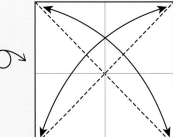

2. Flip the paper over to the other side. Fold the paper diagonally in half in one direction and unfold, then repeat in the other direction.

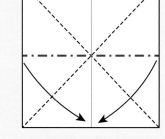

3. Bring the left and right folds diagonally down and inward while folding the top section down as well.

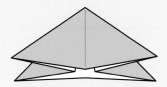

4. This is an origami water bomb base. Flatten the paper.

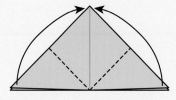

5. Fold the left and right lower points diagonally up to the top point.

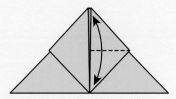

6. Next make a horizontal crease on the right flap by folding the top point down to the bottom and then unfolding it.

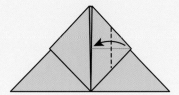

7. Fold the right point to meet the left end of the crease you made in the previous step.

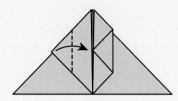

8. Fold the left point to match the right side.

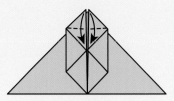

9. Fold the two top points down.

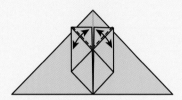

10. Fold the two top points diagonally down and unfold.

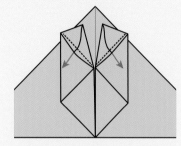

11. Insert the two top flaps down inside the pockets of the flaps underneath.

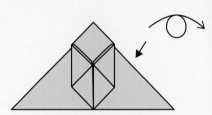

12. Flip the model over and repeat the same process on the other side.

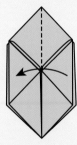

13. Fold the right side over to the left, flip the model over, and repeat on the back so that the model becomes three-dimensional.

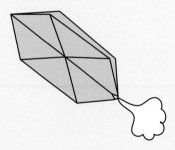

14. Pick up the model and hold it loosely. Blow into the end that has a little opening.

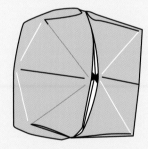

15. While blowing into the model, gently shape the sides into a cube.

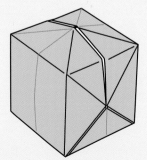

16. You can straighten the edges now if you like.

Tea Bag

This cute little origami tea bag is a perfect gift tag! Or you can use it as a greeting card by writing your message on the tea bag. You can then make a special tea bag envelope (page 22) to send them in. It's best to use white paper or the white side of your paper for this tea bag. The colored side of the paper in the instructions is the back (unseen) side of the paper.

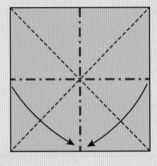

OPTIONAL HEART MATERIALS: 1 × 1–inch (3 × 3–cm) paper + 2 inches (5 cm) of string

DIFFICULTY: ⭐⭐

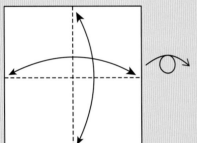

1. Fold the paper in half from top to bottom and unfold, then fold the paper in half from left to right and unfold.

2. Flip the paper over to the other side. Fold the paper diagonally in half in one direction and unfold, then repeat in the other direction.

3. Bring the left and right folds diagonally down and in while folding the top section down as well.

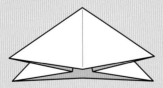

4. This is an origami water bomb base. Flatten the paper.

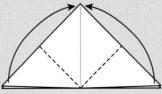

5. Fold the left and right lower points diagonally up to the top point.

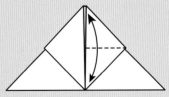

6. Make a horizontal crease on the right flap by folding the top point down to the bottom and unfolding it.

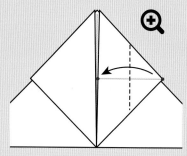

7. Fold the right point to meet the left edge of the crease you made in the previous step.

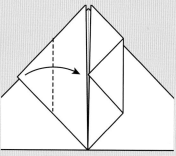

8. Fold the left point to match the right side.

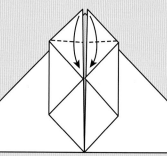

9. Fold the two top points down.

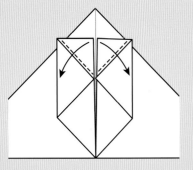

10. Fold the two top points diagonally down.

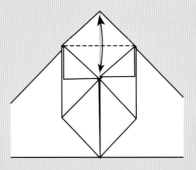

11. Fold the top point down, make a strong crease, and unfold.

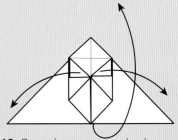

12. Open the paper completely.

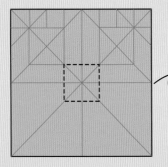

13. With the back of the paper (the colored side in this diagram) facing up, refold the central square shape.

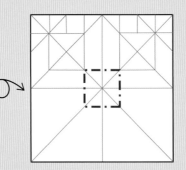

14. Flip the paper over to the front (the white side in this diagram).

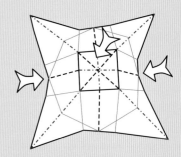

15. Sink fold the small square down inside while re-forming the water bomb base.

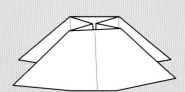

16. Find the two sides of the model that have no extra creases and work with them facing up.

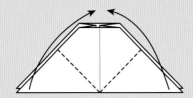

17. Fold the bottom left and right points diagonally up.

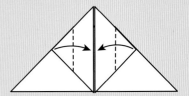

18. Fold the left and right points in to the center.

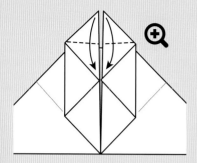

19. Fold the two top points down.

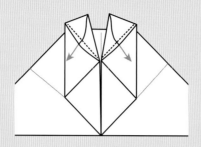

20. Fold the two top points diagonally down and insert them into the pockets of the flaps underneath.

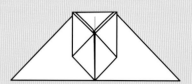

21. Repeat the process on the other side.

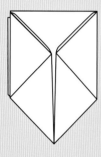

22. Your model should now look like this.

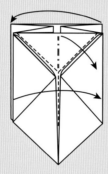

23. Fold the left side over to the right while squashing the upper triangle down. Repeat on the back.

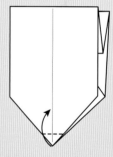

24. Fold the bottom point up a little.

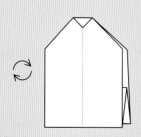

25. Rotate the model.

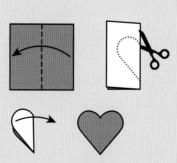

26. To make a little heart for the tag, fold a little square in half, cut out a half-heart shape. Open the paper back up to reveal a perfect heart.

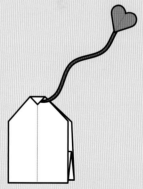

27. You can attach a string to the heart and the tea bag using a dab of glue. Add tea leaves for brewing, or bath salts and herbs for bathing. Steep and enjoy!

Tea Bag Envelopes

These origami envelopes just happen to be the right size to keep your little origami tea bags in! They also make great envelopes in general. Here are two versions of this easy-to-make envelope: the first is the basic version, and the second is a more secure version.

DIFFICULTY:

BASIC VERSION

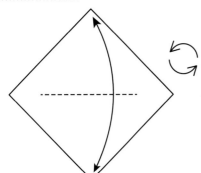

1. Make a horizontal crease by folding the bottom point up to the top point and then unfolding it. Avoid creasing the left and right ends for a cleaner result.

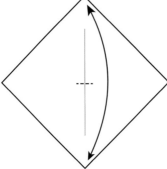

2. Rotate the paper so that the crease you made in the previous step is now vertical. Bring the bottom point up to the top point, make a small crease in the center, and unfold.

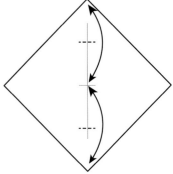

3. Bring the top point and the bottom point to the center, make two small creases, and then unfold.

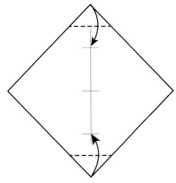

4. Fold the top point and the bottom point to the creases you made in the previous step.

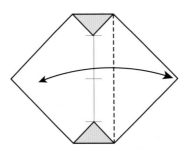

5. Fold the right point over to the left, aligning the diagonal edges to the triangular flaps, and unfold.

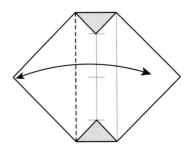

6. Repeat the previous step on the left side.

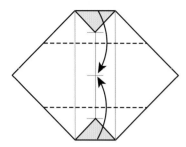

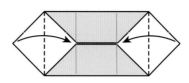

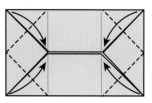

7. Fold the top and bottom edges to the middle.

8. Fold the left and right points to align with the top and bottom sections.

9. Fold all four corners diagonally inward.

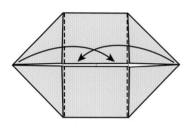

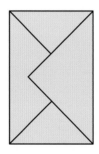

10. Fold the left and right points inward so one overlaps the other.

11. Here's your very own basic origami envelope!

12. You can use ribbon to secure the envelope shut.

SECURE VERSION

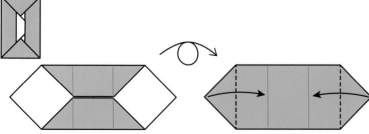

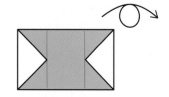

1. Unfold the envelope back to step 8, or fold a new envelope up to step 8.

2. Flip the paper over and fold the left and right points inward.

3. Flip the paper back over.

4. Fold all four corners diagonally inward.

5. Unfold the previous step.

6. Flip the paper over. Make a vertical crease on the left and right triangular flaps as indicated.

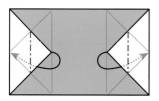

7. Tuck the two creases you created in the previous step behind.

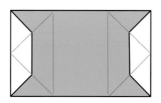

8. Here's how your model should look now.

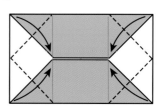

9. Flip the paper over and refold all four corners diagonally inward.

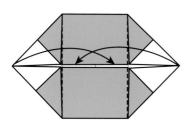

10. Fold the left and the right points inward, so one overlaps the other.

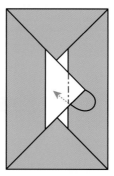

11. Fold the point on the top layer behind and underneath the pocket on the layer behind it.

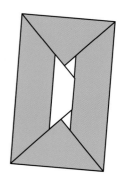

12. Here's your super-secure origami envelope!

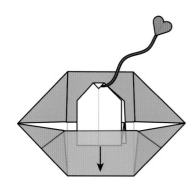

13. You can open your envelope and place an origami tea bag inside the lower pocket, or open the envelope's top section as well to completely secure it inside.

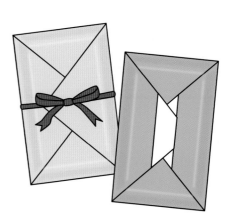

Cute Purse

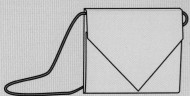

This origami purse is based on the same folding method used for the Kawaii envelopes on page 11. You can use this purse as an envelope too. What makes this one appealing is that it becomes a pouch that can be opened up and will hold items securely. You can make a real purse with this project!

DIFFICULTY:

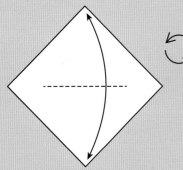

1. Create a horizontal crease by folding the top point down to the bottom point and unfolding it. For a clean finish, avoid creasing the left and right ends.

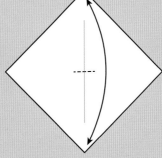

2. Rotate the paper and create a small horizontal crease in the middle using the same method from step 1.

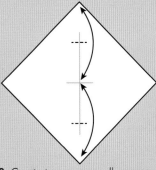

3. Create two more small creases by bringing the top and bottom points to the crease made in the previous step and unfolding them.

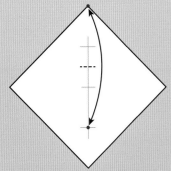

4. Make another small crease by bringing the top point down to the lowest small crease and then unfolding it.

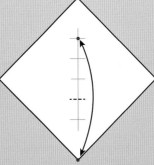

5. Create a final small crease by bringing the bottom point up to the topmost small crease and then unfolding it.

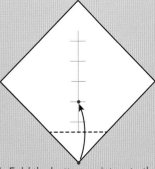

6. Fold the bottom point up to the second crease from the bottom.

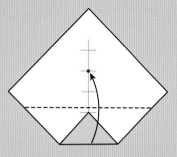

7. Fold the bottom edge up to the second crease from the top.

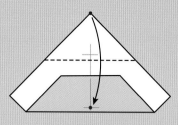

8. Fold the top point down to the small crease at the bottom.

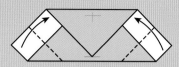

9. Fold the bottom left and right sides diagonally up to meet the edges of the top triangle.

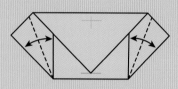

10. Create diagonal creases on the left and right sides by folding and unfolding the right and left edges.

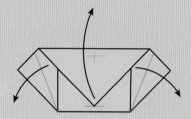

11. Unfold the top section and then unfold the left and right flaps.

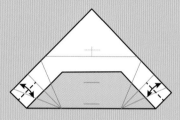

12. Create a diagonal crease where indicated on the left and right sides by folding and unfolding the right and left edges.

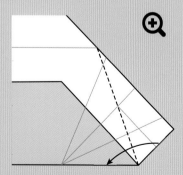

13. Create a diagonal crease where indicated on the right side of the paper by folding the right edge . . .

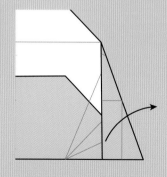

14. . . . and unfolding it.

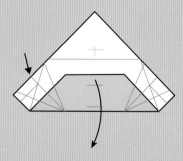

15. Repeat the previous two steps on the left side. Unfold the bottom section downward.

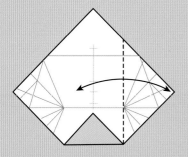

16. Fold the right section over to the left, aligning its diagonal edge to the diagonal edge of the bottom triangle. Unfold.

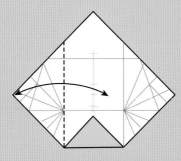

17. Repeat the previous step on the left side.

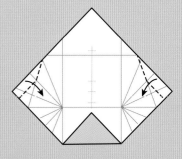

18. Refold the creases indicated on the left and right.

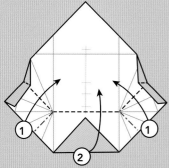

19. Next bring the points marked 1 up and diagonally in, followed by the lower edge, which is marked 2.

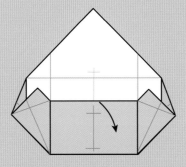

20. Flatten the paper and then open the bottom section so that you can get to the flaps underneath.

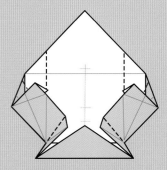

21. Use the existing creases that are indicated here . . .

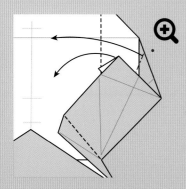

22. . . . and bring the right section to the left while using the crease indicated by the red dot as a mountain fold as indicated.

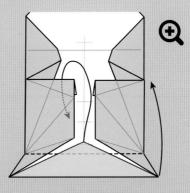

23. Repeat on the left side, then bring the bottom section back up and slot the triangular flap down inside the pocket.

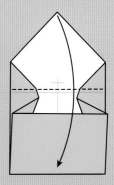

24. Now you can fold the top point down to the bottom, creating a new horizontal crease . . .

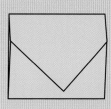

25. . . . and your purse will look like this.

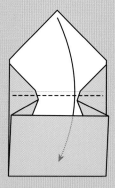

26. Or you can slot the point inside the envelope to secure it.

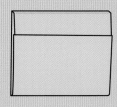

27. Then your purse will look like this.

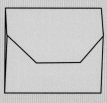

28. You could even fold the point underneath to make the flap look more rounded.

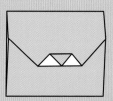

29. Or fold the flap up a little, then fold it down to make a little design. No matter what you do, it'll be cute!

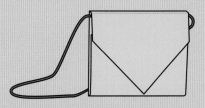

30. To use this model as a purse, you can glue or sew some ribbon underneath the flap.

This purse will go perfectly with my outfit!

Cat & Dog Hearts

Perfect for either the cat or dog lover in your life, these adorable little pets can be decorated with all kinds of cute Kawaii faces. They are perfect for a peek-a-boo "hello!" token gift. Try using complementary colors for the heart to go with their faces.

DIFFICULTY:

CAT VERSION

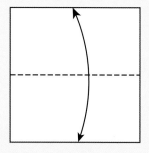

1. Starting with your paper white side up, fold the paper in half vertically and unfold.

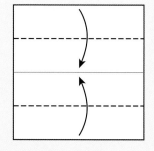

2. Fold the top and bottom edges to meet the crease you made in the previous step.

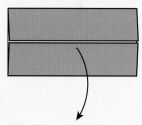

3. Open the lower section.

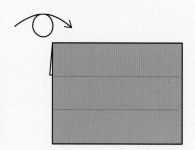

4. Flip the paper over to the other side from left to right.

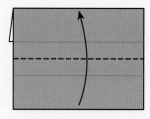

5. Fold the bottom edge up to the top edge.

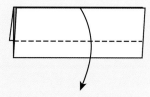

6. Fold the top edge back down along the existing crease as indicated.

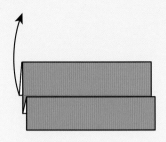

7. Unfold the top section back up from behind.

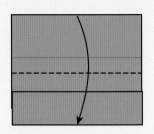

8. Fold the top edge down to the bottom edge.

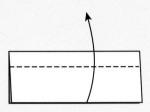

9. Fold the flap back up along the existing crease.

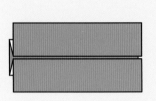

10. Rotate the paper.

11. Here is what your model should now look like.

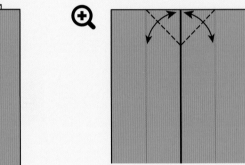

12. Create diagonal creases on the inner corners of the top left and right sections.

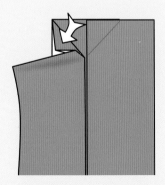

13. Reverse fold the left diagonal crease.

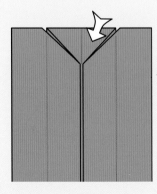

14. Reverse fold the right diagonal crease.

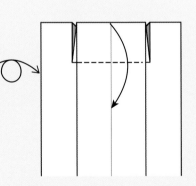

15. Flip the model over to the other side. Fold the top central section down, leaving the left and right sections in place.

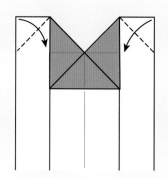

16. Fold the top left and right corners down diagonally.

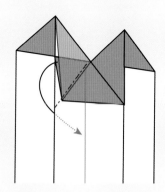

17. You can fold the inner corner down inside the central section, but only if your paper allows it.

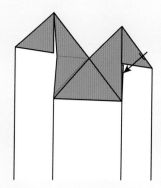

18. Repeat on the right.

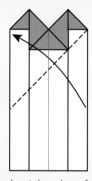

19. Bring the right edge of the paper diagonally up to the left, aligning it with the top left horizontal edge of the top triangular flap.

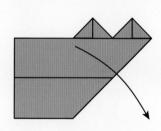

20. Unfold.

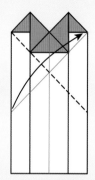

21. Repeat step 19 on the left side.

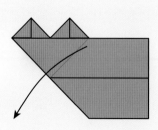

22. Unfold.

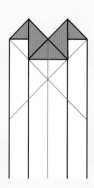

23. Here is what your model should now look like.

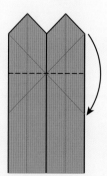

24. Flip the paper over to the other side. Fold the top section down, so that the two diagonal creases meet each other.

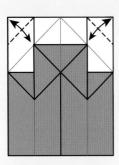

25. Fold and unfold to create diagonal creases on the top left and right corners.

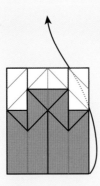

26. Bring the bottom flap up from behind.

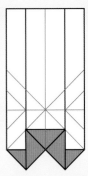

27. This is what your model should now look like. Focus on the lower section.

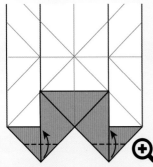

28. Fold the bottom left and right points up.

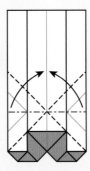

29. Bring the left and right edges up, collapsing the lower section up at the same time.

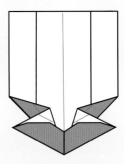

30. This is what your model should now look like.

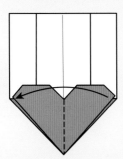

31. Flip the right section of the emerging heart shape over to the left.

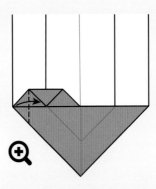

32. Fold the far-left point over to the right.

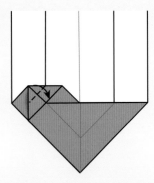

33. Fold the top left point diagonally down to complete the left side of the heart shape.

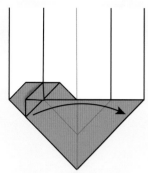

34. Fold the section back over to the right.

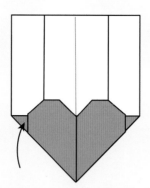

35. Repeat steps 31 to 34 on the left section of the heart.

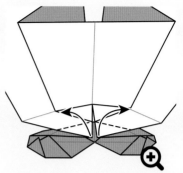

36. Look inside the heart and fold the two inner points behind, along the existing creases.

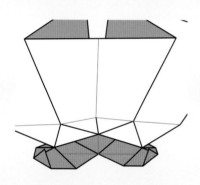

37. This is what your model should now look like inside.

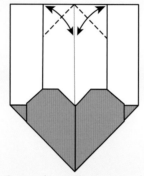

38. Create diagonal creases on the left and right corners of the central section as indicated.

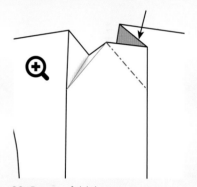

39. Reverse fold the creases you made in the previous step.

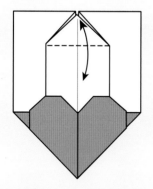

40. Fold the top point of the top central section down and back up again to create a crease.

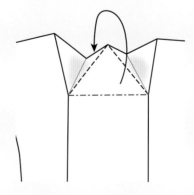

41. Open the top section a little, fold the central point down inside, and close it again.

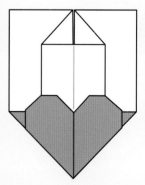

42. This is what your model should now look like.

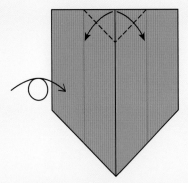

43. Flip the model over to the other side. Diagonally fold the left and right corners of the central section as indicated.

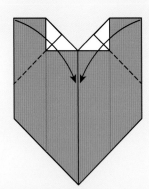

44. Diagonally fold the left and right edges inward to meet the vertical crease.

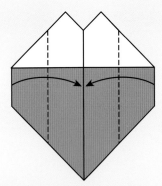

45. Fold the left and right edges in for a final time.

DOG VERSION

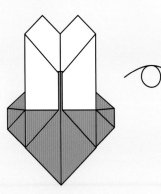

46. This is what your model should now look like.

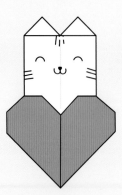

47. Flip the model over to the other side, and draw or use stickers to create an adorable kitty face! Or . . .

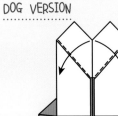

1. On the back of the heart, fold the two "ears" down diagonally.

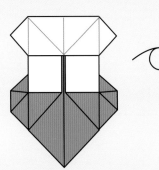

2. This is what your model should now look like.

3. Flip the model back over to the other side and draw or add stickers to create the face of a real cute pooch!

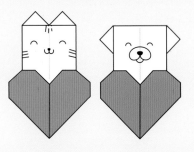

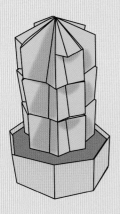

Cactus

This fun origami project is not sharp and is a perfect gift for your friend who cannot take care of a real plant—no watering is necessary! You can even make a couple of these origami cacti and stack them on top of each other to create different heights! Try different greens as well to give depth and variety.

DIFFICULTY:

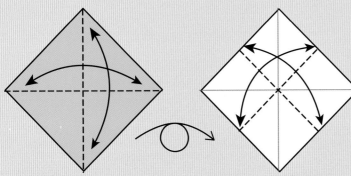

1. Starting with your paper color side up, create vertical and horizontal creases by folding and unfolding the paper in half top to bottom and then left to right.

2. Flip the paper over. Create diagonal creases by folding and unfolding the paper in half diagonally in both directions.

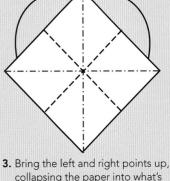

3. Bring the left and right points up, collapsing the paper into what's known as an origami square base.

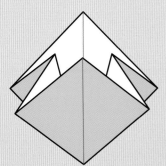

4. Flatten the paper, making sure that the open end is at the top.

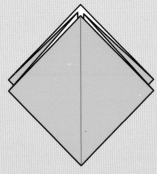

5. This is what your model should now look like.

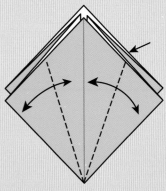

6. Fold the left and right lower diagonal edges to the central vertical crease and unfold. Repeat this on the back.

Cactus   39

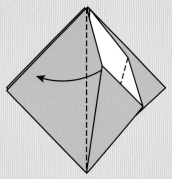

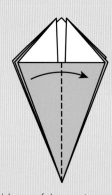

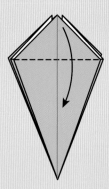

7. Open one of the flaps and squash the paper as indicated. Repeat this on all of the other flaps.

8. Fold one of the sections over so that you are viewing a solid kite shape.

9. Fold the top point down. Repeat on all sides.

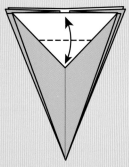

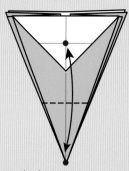

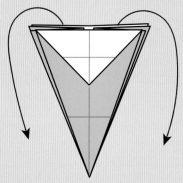

10. Fold the bottom point of the top triangular flap up to the top edge and unfold.

11. Bring the bottom point up to meet the point indicated by the red dot, crease well, and unfold.

12. Open up the paper completely to the white side.

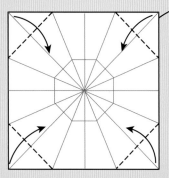

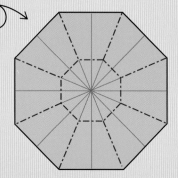

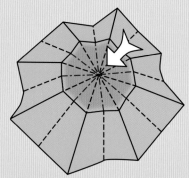

13. Fold all four points inward along the existing creases.

14. Flip the paper over to the other side. Make all of the creases indicated in red into mountain folds.

15. Pick up the paper and carefully sink fold the octagon shape down inside.

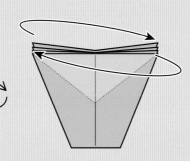
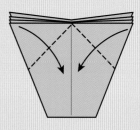

16. This is what your model should now look like.

17. Rotate and flatten the paper. Make sure that a triangular flap is behind the top layer you are working on.

18. Fold the top left and top right points diagonally down to align with the central vertical crease.

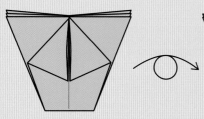
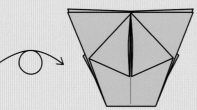
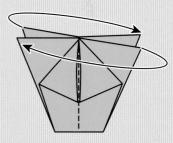

19. This is what your model should now look like.

20. Flip the paper over and repeat on the back, making sure you have equal flaps on each side.

21. Flip the sections so that you can repeat step 18 on the remaining flaps.

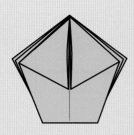
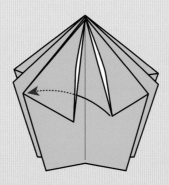
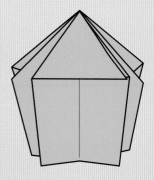

22. This is what your model should now look like.

23. Insert the right flap inside the left flap, making the model three-dimensional.

24. Repeat the previous step on all the sides.

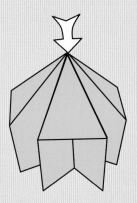

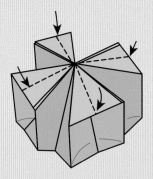

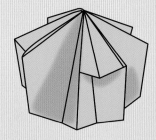

25. You can push the top point down to give the cactus a four-leaf clover shape.

26. You can push the top flaps down, creating valley folds, and squash them, giving the cactus a pointier look.

27. If you are using small paper, you may want to use a dab of glue to secure the cactus sections together once you make more of them. Image shown has three sections on a round pot.

We don't need to water these!

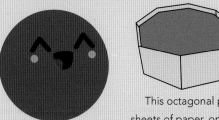

Round Pot

This octagonal pot is perfect to use as a base for our cactus project on page 39. We will use two sheets of paper, one for the outside of the pot and one for the inside. The paper for the inside part needs to be a tiny bit smaller than the paper used for the outside. This project uses the same method as the traditional masu box on page 8. If you are using 6 × 6–inch (15 × 15–cm) paper for the pot, then:

POT PAPER SIZE: 6 × 6 (15 × 15 cm)

SOIL PAPER SIZE: Cut to 5.7 × 5.7 (14.5 × 14.5 cm)

DIFFICULTY:

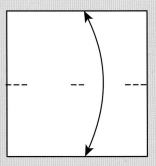

1. Start by creating horizontal creases where indicated by folding and unfolding the paper.

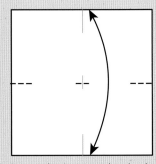

2. Rotate the paper and make the same horizontal creases.

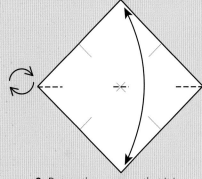

3. Rotate the paper so that it is oriented as shown and create the same horizontal creases.

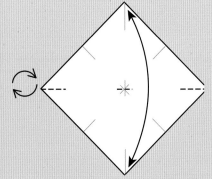

4. Again rotate the paper and create a final set of horizontal creases.

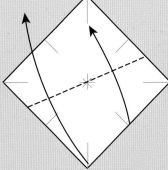

5. Fold the bottom right diagonal edge up so that the creases match as shown here.

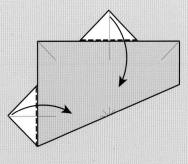

6. Fold the bottom left and top points over the front flap.

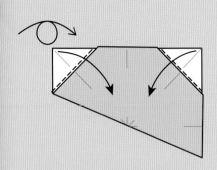

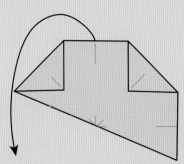

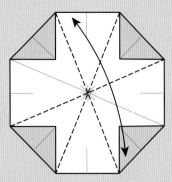

7. Flip the paper over from left to right, and fold the top left and right points forward.

8. Open the paper, but leave the corners folded.

9. You should now have an octagonal shape. One of the diagonal creases is already completed; now create matching folds where indicated.

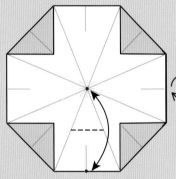

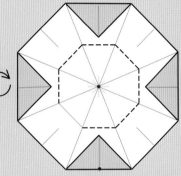

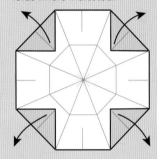

10. Bring the bottom edge to the center point and make a crease where indicated.

11. Rotate the paper and repeat the previous step on all eight sides.

12. Rotate the paper and open up the four corner flaps.

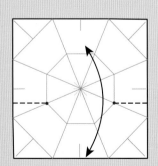

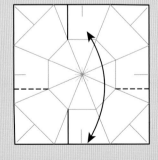

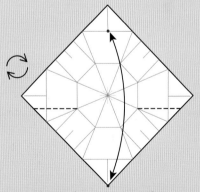

13. Make horizontal creases where indicated, avoiding the middle.

14. Rotate the paper and repeat the creases on the other three sides.

15. Rotate the paper. Bring the bottom point up to the point indicated by the red dot and unfold, creating the horizontal creases indicated. Keep avoiding the middle.

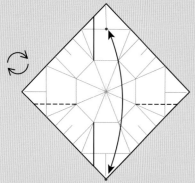

16. Rotate the paper and repeat the previous step on the other three sides.

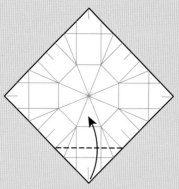

17. Using the existing creases as a guide, fold the bottom corner up.

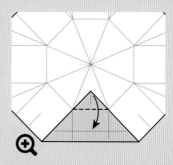

18. Fold the top point of the triangular flap down as indicated.

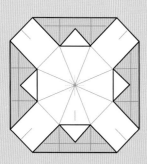

19. Repeat the last two steps on the other three points.

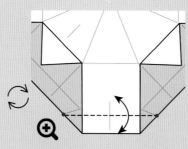

20. Rotate the paper and fold the bottom edge up from the points indicated by the red dots.

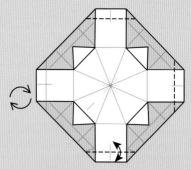

21. Rotate the paper and repeat the previous step on the other three edges.

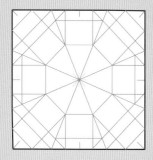

22. Open up the paper all the way.

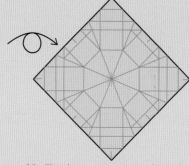

23. Flip the paper over to the color side and rotate it as indicated.

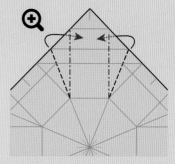

24. Focus on the top point. Pick up the paper and fold along the creases as indicated, making the pot three-dimensional.

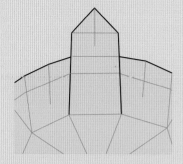

25. This is what the point should now look like. Repeat on the other three points.

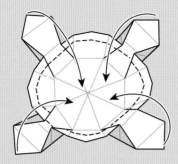

26. Looking at the pot from above, collapse all four points over and into the pot.

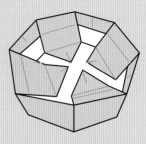

27. Straighten out the flaps inside the pot.

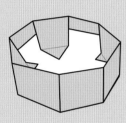

28. This is what your finished outside pot will look like.

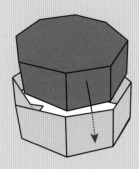

29. Create a second pot from slightly smaller paper and insert it upside down inside the larger pot.

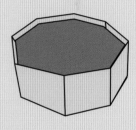

30. Here is your completed pot!

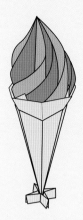

Ice-Cream Cone

This pretty, three-dimensional origami ice-cream cone almost looks like the real thing! You can use one or two colors of paper for the ice cream, depending on if you want one "flavor" or two.

ICE-CREAM CONE PAPER: 3 to 4 sheets of 6 × 6 inches (15 × 15 cm)

OPTIONAL ICE-CREAM CONE STAND PAPER SIZE: 2 × 2 inches (5 × 5 cm)

DIFFICULTY:

OUTER CONE

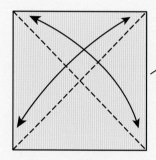

1. With the color side up, fold and unfold the paper in half diagonally in both directions.

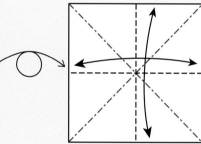

2. Flip the paper over and fold and unfold the paper in half top to bottom and left to right.

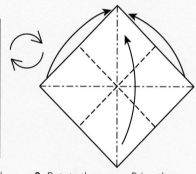

3. Rotate the paper. Bring the left, right, and bottom points up using the creases made in the previous steps.

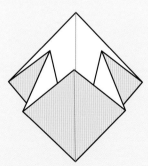

4. Flatten the paper into an origami square base with the open end at the top.

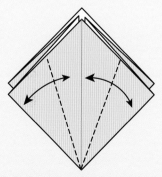

5. Fold the left and right diagonal edges to the central vertical crease and unfold. Repeat on the back.

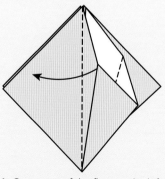

6. Open one of the flaps to the left, squashing the center. Repeat on all of the other sides.

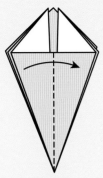

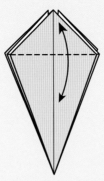

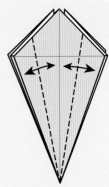

7. Fold one of the flaps to the right so that you are looking at a kite shape.

8. Fold the top point down and back up again. Repeat this step on all of the other sides.

9. Fold the left and right sides to the central vertical crease and unfold. Repeat on all sides.

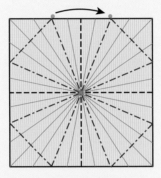

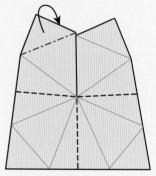

10. Unfold the paper completely, laying it down with the colored side up.

11. Reinforce all of the creases using mountain and valley folds as indicated. Pick up the paper and bring the left point indicated over to the right point indicated.

12. Fold the top left point over and behind. Repeat steps 11 and 12 on the other points until you have a closed cone.

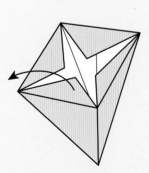

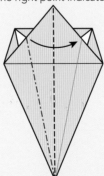

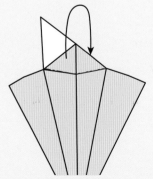

13. Holding the cone, open one of the flaps.

14. Using the existing crease on the left as a mountain fold, bring it over to the right crease that is indicated.

15. Fold the top flap over and down inside the cone along the indicated crease.

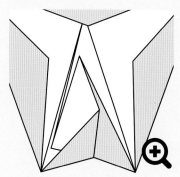

16. If you look inside the cone, this is what you should have.

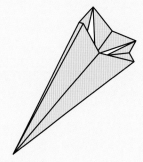

17. Here's your yummy cone!

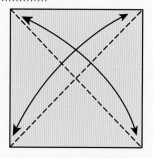

1. With the color side facing up, fold and unfold the paper diagonally in both directions.

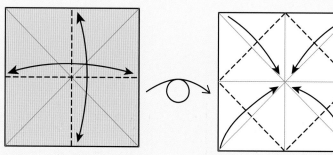

2. Fold and unfold the paper in half top to bottom and left to right.

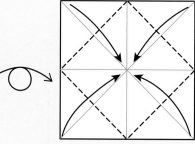

3. Flip the paper over and fold all four corners to the center.

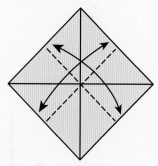

4. Fold and unfold the paper diagonally in half in both directions.

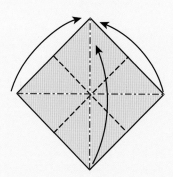

5. Bring the left, right, and bottom points up to the top.

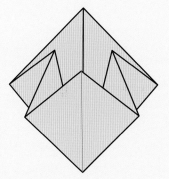

6. Flatten the paper into an origami square base with the open end at the top.

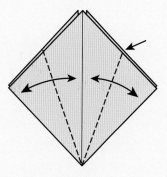

7. Fold the lower left and right diagonal edges to the central vertical crease and unfold. Repeat on the back.

Ice-Cream Cone   51

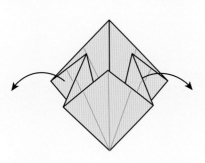

8. Open the paper back up to step 4.

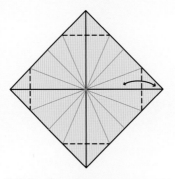

9. Using the existing creases as a guide, fold all four corners inward and unfold.

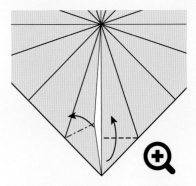

10. Focus on the bottom point of the paper. Using the existing fold, open the left side of the corner while pushing the right side of the corner up.

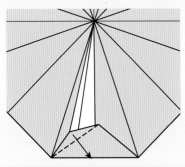

11. Push the left side of the flap back down on top.

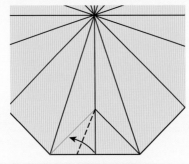

12. Make the indicated diagonal crease on the left section.

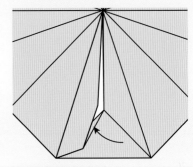

13. Reverse the fold you created in the previous step so it sits inside. Repeat steps 10 to 13 on all the other corners.

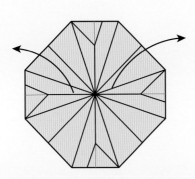

14. Open the paper up completely with the colored side facing up.

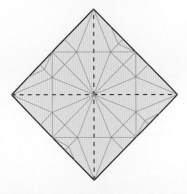

15. Refold the indicated creases.

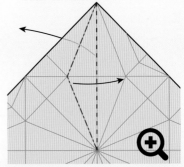

16. Focusing on the top corner, bring the indicated mountain folds over to the right in a similar manner to the outer cone.

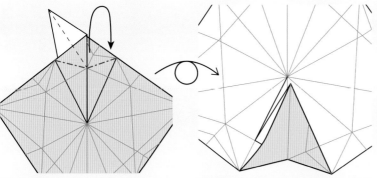
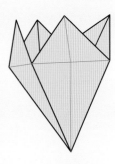

17. Fold the top section down and behind along the indicated creases.

18. Flip the paper over to make sure that it is folded correctly (it should look like this).

19. Repeat steps 16–18 on the other three corners. Here is how your inner cone should now look.

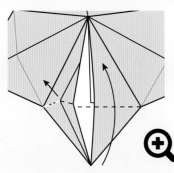

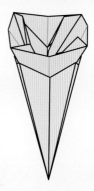

20. Refold steps 10 to 13 on each point of the cone.

21. Apply a dab of glue on the lower part of the inner cone.

22. Slot the inner cone into the outer cone. Allow the glue time to dry.

ICE CREAM

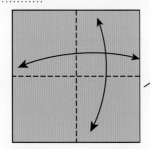
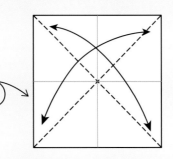
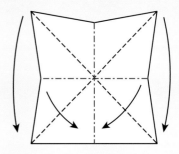

1. With the color side up, fold and unfold the paper in half top to bottom and left to right.

2. Flip the paper over and fold and unfold it in half diagonally in both directions.

3. Bring the top left and right points down while pushing the left and right central points inward.

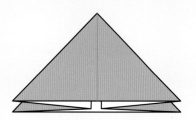

4. Now you have an origami water bomb base.

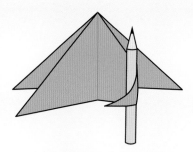

5. Use something cylindrical, such as a pencil, to curl a flap in a clockwise direction.

6. Continue to curl each of the flaps clockwise.

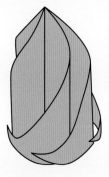

7. You've got some great ice cream! You can slot this into the inner flaps of the cone (see step 10) and enjoy it just as it is, or . . .

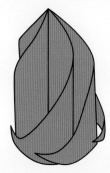

8. . . . if you are having two "flavors," repeat steps 1 to 6 using your second sheet of paper.

FLAVOR TIP

For a fuller-looking ice cream, use another sheet of paper that is the same color. Or for ice cream that is two "flavors," use another sheet of a different color.

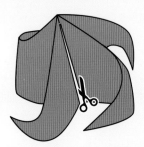

9. Open the second ice cream up a bit and cut slots as indicated on each side without cutting all the way to the top.

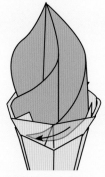

10. Slot the first ice cream flavor into the inner flaps of the cone.

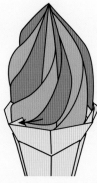

11. Slot the second flavor (if using) over the top, in between each section of the first flavor, and into the small flaps you created in step 20 of the inner cone.

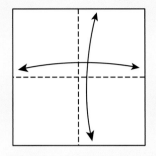

1. Fold and unfold your paper in half top to bottom and left to right.

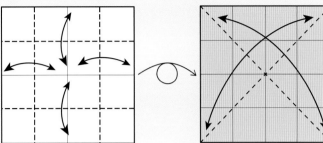

2. Fold each edge of the paper to the middle and unfold.

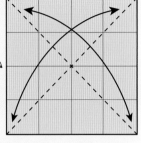

3. Flip the paper over and fold and unfold the paper in half diagonally in both directions.

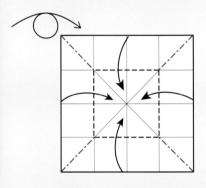

4. Flip the paper back over and bring the left, right, top, and bottom edges inward while also bringing each corner to the center.

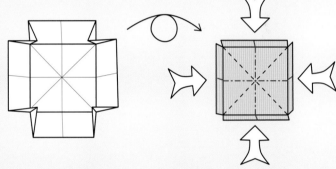
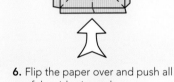

5. Here is what your model should now look like.

6. Flip the paper over and push all of the sides inward.

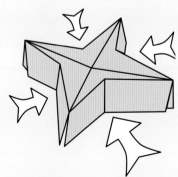

7. Continue pushing the sides until you have an "X" shape.

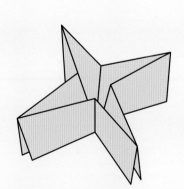

8. Here is the stand for your delicious ice-cream cone!

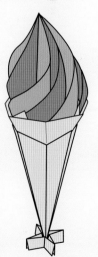

Ice-Cream Cone 55

Sushi Roll Boxes

These cute little boxes look like sliced sushi rolls! You can make a few of them for a fun Japanese snack display, along with a cute wasabi (page 15) or add a sticker face to create a cute character.

SUSHI ROLL BOX PAPER SIZE: 6 × 6 inches (15 × 15 cm)

OUTER MASU BOX PAPER SIZE: 4 × 4 inches (10 × 10 cm)

DIFFICULTY:

SUSHI ROLL BOX LID

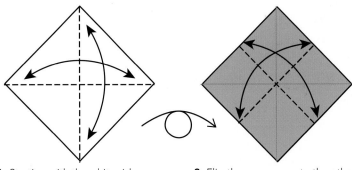

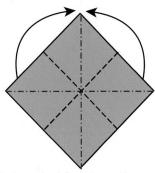

1. Starting with the white side up, fold the paper in half in both directions and unfold.

2. Flip the paper over to the other side. Fold the paper diagonally in half in both directions and unfold.

3. Bring the left, right, and bottom points up to the top.

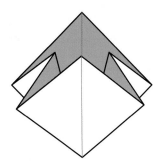
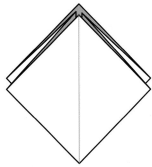
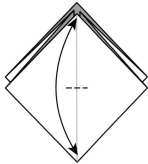

4. Flatten the paper to form an origami square base.

5. Make sure the open end is at the top.

6. Create a small horizontal crease by folding the top point down to the bottom point and unfolding it.

Sushi Roll Boxes   57

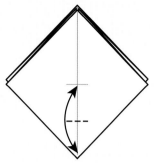

7. Fold the bottom point up to the crease you created in the previous step, make a small crease, and unfold.

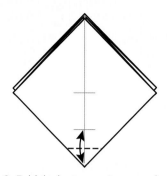

8. Fold the bottom point up to the crease you made in the previous step, crease well, and unfold.

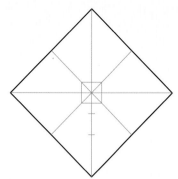

9. Open up the paper completely.

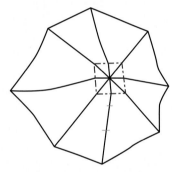

10. Pick up the paper and refold the small square shape in the middle as mountain folds.

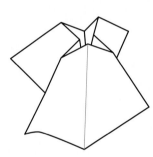

11. Sink fold the small square down inside while re-forming the square base.

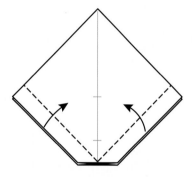

12. Flatten the paper and rotate. Fold the top layer of the lower left and right diagonal edges up as indicated.

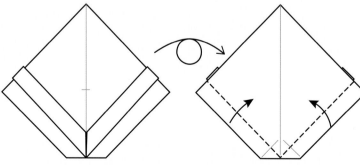

13. This is how your model should now look.

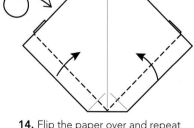

14. Flip the paper over and repeat step 12 on this side.

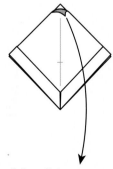

15. Carefully pull the topmost layer down while keeping the diagonal flaps folded.

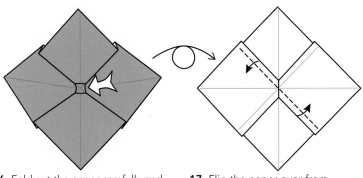

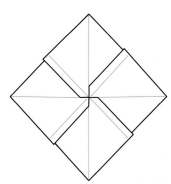

16. Fold out the paper carefully and flatten the central square shape.

17. Flip the paper over from left to right. Fold the top left diagonal flap and bottom right diagonal flap as indicated.

18. Here's what your model should now look like.

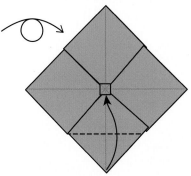

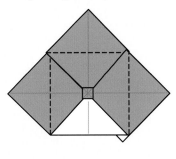

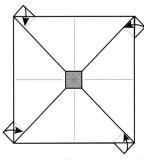

19. Flip the model over from left to right and fold the bottom point up and underneath the square shape, making sure the edges are aligned.

20. Here's how your model should look. Rotate the paper and repeat the previous step on all the sides. You can glue these flaps down if you like.

21. Tuck the small corners in and slot them underneath.

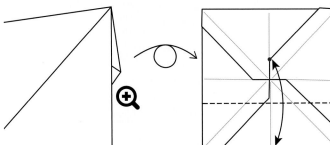

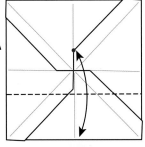

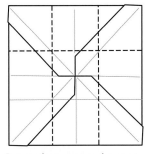

22. Here's a close-up of what the corners should look like.

23. Flip the paper over to the other side. Fold the bottom edge up to the point indicated and unfold.

24. Rotate the paper and repeat the previous step on the other three sides.

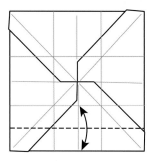

25. Fold the bottom edge up to the horizontal crease that is indicated and unfold.

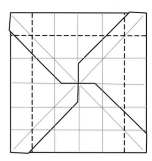

26. Repeat the previous step on the other three sides.

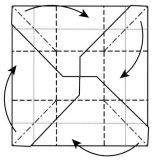

27. Lift all four points up and rotate them clockwise, making the box three-dimensional.

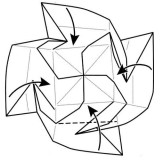

28. While holding the box in shape, fold the lower edges over and inside the box.

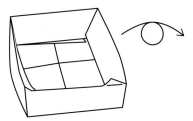

29. Here's how your box should look.

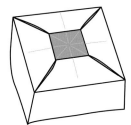

30. Flip the box over.

31. Next make a masu box (page 8) using paper that is two-thirds the size of the paper you used for the sushi roll box lid. Put the sushi roll box lid inside the masu box and enjoy!

VARIATION

For a more advanced, cleaner version, use paper with white on both sides.

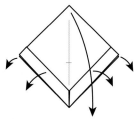

1. Fold up to step 14 of the sushi roll box lid, except this time unfold the paper completely.

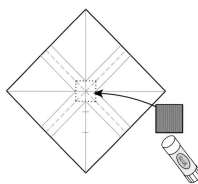

2. There is a small square shape in the center of the paper. Glue on a square of colored paper here . . .

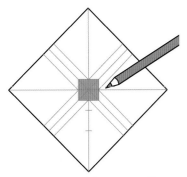

. . . or you could use a pencil to color the square in.

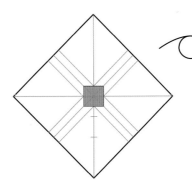

3. Here is your paper.

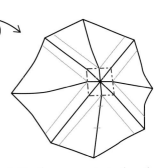

4. Flip the paper over to the other side and sink fold the small square.

5. Here is what your model should now look like.

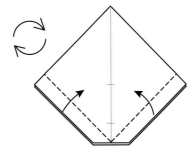

6. Flatten and rotate the paper so that the opening is at the top and refold the lower diagonal creases on the front and back.

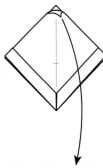

7. Carefully pull the top layer down while keeping the diagonal flaps in place.

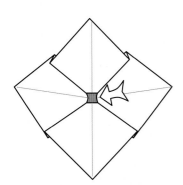

8. Carefully flatten the paper including the little square in the middle.

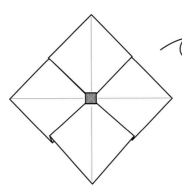

9. Here is what your model should now look like.

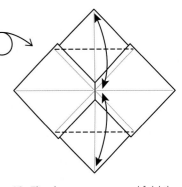

10. Flip the paper over and fold the top and bottom points to the middle and unfold.

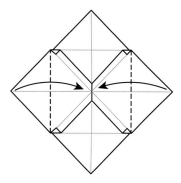

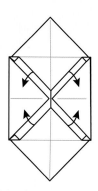

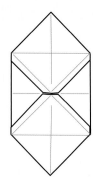

11. Fold the left and right points to the center.

12. Fold the four inner diagonal flaps as indicated.

13. Here is what your model should now look like.

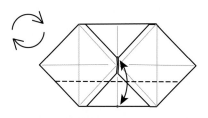

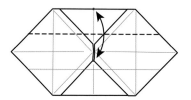

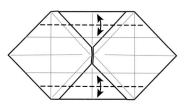

14. Rotate the paper. Fold the bottom edge to the point indicated by the red dot and unfold.

15. Fold the top edge to the point indicated by the red dot and unfold.

16. Fold the top and bottom edges to the two creases you just made and unfold.

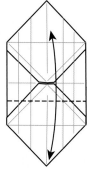

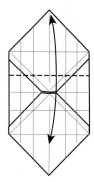

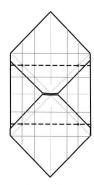

17. Rotate the paper. Create a new horizontal crease that runs through the points indicated by the red dots.

18. Create another new horizontal crease that runs through the points indicated by the red dots.

19. Create two more horizontal creases where indicated by the red dots.

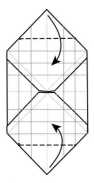

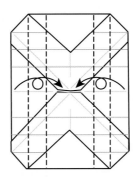

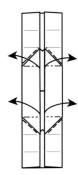

20. Using the two outermost vertical creases as a guide, fold the top and bottom points inward.

21. Using the existing creases, fold the left and right edges in twice to the middle.

22. Create diagonal folds where indicated, with the same method used for closing the traditional masu box on page 8. Open up the left and right flaps in the center, making the box three-dimensional.

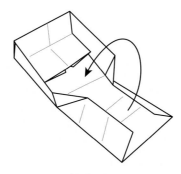

23. Close the top of the box by bringing the top flap down and inside the box.

24. Insert the lower section into the inside of the box.

25. You can use a dab of glue to secure the flaps inside if you like.

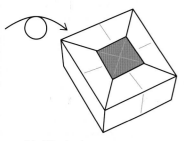

These are so adorable!

26. Flip the box over.

27. Make a masu box (page 8) using paper that is two-thirds the size of the paper you used to create this variation of the sushi roll box lid. Put the sushi roll box lid inside the masu box and give yourself a pat on the back!

Thunder Bay Press
An imprint of Printers Row Publishing Group
A division of Readerlink Distribution Services, LLC
10350 Barnes Canyon Road, Suite 100, San Diego, CA 92121
www.thunderbaybooks.com • mail@thunderbaybooks.com

Printers Row Publishing Group is a division of Readerlink Distribution Services, LLC. Thunder Bay Press is a registered trademark of Readerlink Distribution Services, LLC.

This 2020 edition is published by Thunder Bay Press in arrangement with Race Point Publishing, and contains text previously published in *Kawaii Origami*, © 2019.

Correspondence regarding the content of this book should be sent to Thunder Bay Press, Editorial Department, at the above address. Author, illustration, and rights inquiries should be addressed to Race Point Publishing, The Quarto Group, 142 W. 36th St, 4th Floor, New York, NY 10018; 212-779-4972; www.quartoknows.com.

Thunder Bay Press
Publisher: Peter Norton • Associate Publisher: Ana Parker
Editor: JoAnn Padgett
Senior Product Manager: Kathryn C. Dalby

Editorial Director: Rage Kindelsperger
Creative Director: Laura Drew
Managing Editor: Cara Donaldson
Senior Editor: John Foster
Art Director: Cindy Samargia Laun
Interior Design and Layout: Ashley Prine, Tandem Books
Cover Design and Additional Layout: Kim Winscher

Kawaii faces and difficulty stars © RedKoala/Shutterstock
Speech bubbles © MisterEmil/Shutterstock

ISBN: 978-1-64517-382-3

Printed, manufactured, and assembled in Guangdong, China

24 23 22 21 20   1 2 3 4 5